Witty Alfie
BONUS ACCESS

Join our fun club and get bonus monthly access to our giveaways & extras !

All you need to do is send us an email to WAPublishingGroup@gmail.com with the title "AMAZING ALFIE" — submit one ridiculous "Would You Rather..?" question and get :

- An entry to our monthly giveaway to win 50$ Amazon Gift Card !

- Access to our **free extras** !

A winner with the best submission will be picked each month and will be contacted via email.

Best of Luck !

'Laughter is timeless, imagination has no age and dreams are forever' - Walt Disney

A child's imagination knows no boundaries. Children have an innate ability to imagine and create stories from scratch and are always looking for new ideas and experiences to understand the world around them.

These "Would You Rather? - Ridiculousness Edition" questions will stimulate your kids' imagination and bring out some amazingly insightful, funny and interesting answers.

This book is a great tool to :

• **Improve communication** by encouraging your children to talk and express themselves freely while discussing their choices in a fun and light-hearted way.

• **Encourage critical thinking** : these questions will help children develop hypotheses about the different scenarios and encourage them to think in new and different ways.

• **Stimulate imagination and creative thinking** through our list of ridiculous and original scenarios.

• **Strengthen relationships** by spurring healthy and interactive discussion in a fun and care-free environment.

• **Nurture curiosity and improve general knowledge** with our list of unique and quite "random" facts.

These questions are an excellent idea to get the conversation started!

Welcome !

Thank you for purchasing my book!

My name is Alfie, I'm an indie author and a full time parent.
I've been working on creating fun and educational games, stories and books for kids for the past couple of years.

As a parent of two, finding ways to entertain the kids while teaching them how to think, communicate and learn important values has been one of my top priorities.
Developing curiosity and creative imagination has become crucial to adapt and grow in today's society.

I really hope you enjoy this book, and if you do, please consider leaving us a review sharing your experience, I'd love to read it and I'd really appreciate it!

Meet Alfie!

He's a sweet and cuddly friend! He gets usually shy around new people, but once he gets to know you, he will become your best companion!

Alfie lives a lot of wacky and crazy adventures, and has an offbeat sense of humor, never failing to offer a good gag or to provoke laughter. Alfie enjoys the simple things in life, like cakes, toys and other squeaky things.

But most importantly, he loves making his friends laugh with his silly, ridiculous jokes and hilarious puns. He likes to cuddle and spend time with the people he cares about the most.

How to Play ?

- *Play with minimum two players* : *Choose at least one other player besides yourself to play the game. If you have a large group of people, you can play around in a circle or even form teams.*

- *Choose the first player who will ask a question that begins with "Would you rather...?" and provide the two scenarios for the second player to choose from.*

- *The second player has to choose <u>only one scenario</u> — and explain why ?*

- *Read the facts, go over the previous questions again and see if the answers will change!*

- *<u>REMEMBER !</u> the questions and scenarios presented in this book are solely for entertainment purposes, and should not be taken seriously !*

Most importantly, have fun, laugh and enjoy your time with your family and loved ones!

WOULD YOU RATHER ?

be able to walk
through walls
or...
be able to see through
walls?

have to ride a unicorn
or...
a dragon to school
everyday?

WOULD YOU RATHER ?

own an elephant-sized chinchilla

or...

a chinchilla-sized elephant?

eat onion-flavored cookies

or..

chicken-flavored ice cream?

WOULD YOU RATHER ?

burp every time
you wink
or...
fart every time you
laugh?

be the shortest person
in the world
or..
the tallest person
in the world ?

WOULD YOU RATHER ?

be able to read
people's mind
or...
have the power to be
invisible?

eat a whole raw potato
or...
a lemon ?

WOULD YOU RATHER ?

*live deep down
in the ocean
or...
live on the clouds for
the rest of your life ?*

*visit the moon once
or...
live in your favorite
place for the rest of
your life ?*

Did You Know...?

- *There are existent camera technologies that make it actually possible to see through walls, mainly used by military and law enforcement.*

- *On 1st of April 2019, KFC introduced a chicken flavored ice cream, but remember to always check the date !*

- *Raw potatoes are more likely to clash with your digestive system and may contain more antinutrients and harmful compounds.*

- *The shortest person in the world measured 21.51 in (54.64 cm) while the tallest person in the world measured 2.72 m (8 ft 11.1 in) tall.*

WOULD YOU RATHER ?

be sprayed with silly string all over your body

or...

have a pie smashed onto your face?

have the ability to teleport wherever you want

or...

the ability to summon anything you want in front of you?

WOULD YOU RATHER ?

> *eat pizza for breakfast*
> *or...*
> *milk and cereals for*
> *dinner for the rest*
> *of your life?*

> *turn into a frog for a*
> *day once a week*
> *or...*
> *a random animal for 2*
> *hours everyday?*

WOULD YOU RATHER ?

go to school wearing an
underwear on your head
or...
wearing one of your
parents' shoes?

become a grown up
tomorrow
or...
stay the age you are
now for 10 years?

WOULD YOU RATHER ?

> *have a flying magic carpet*
> *or...*
> *an all-glass submarine?*

> *hug everyone in the room for 5 minutes*
> *or...*
> *go outside and hug a tree for 10 minutes?*

WOULD YOU RATHER ?

lick the wall
or...
put hot sauce on
ice cream and eat it?

be incredibly lucky
or...
incredibly smart?

Did You Know...?

- *The Challenger Deep in the Mariana Trench is the deepest point recorded in Earth's oceans at a record depth of 10,994 meters (6.831 miles) below sea level.*

- *A spacecraft takes about 3 days to reach the Moon. The distance traveled is around 240,000 miles (386,400 kilometers) which is on average the distance between the Moon and Earth.*

- *Human teleportation is physically impossible, according to Einstein' Theory of special relativity,*

WOULD YOU RATHER ?

be able to remember everyday of your life
or...
to see the future but have no memory?

only be able to run on a potato sack
or...
only be able to move riding a unicycle?

WOULD YOU RATHER ?

have a pause button
or...
a rewind button
in your life?

have the power
to create fire
or...
water?

WOULD YOU RATHER ?

own a giant robot
or...
flying boat?

live in a house in
the shape of a triangle
or...
a circle?

WOULD YOU RATHER ?

> *have to dance
> or...
> sing every morning
> you wake up?*

> *have a giraffe neck
> or...
> an elephant trunk?*

WOULD YOU RATHER ?

have dinner with
Frankenstein
or...
Dracula?

be in kindergarten
or...
first grade forever?

Did You Know...?

- *Hyperthymesia is a condition that leads people to be able to recall almost everyday of their lives in vivid detail. Only 10 people have been recorded to have this condition.*

- *Thanks to its trunk, an elephant sports a sense of smell up to four times as sensitive as a bloodhound's, one of the best detective dog breeds.*

- *Stephen Wildish (UK) holds the record for the fastest 100 meters sack race recorded at 26.22 seconds in Swindon, UK, on 27 October 2017 - Stephen describes himself as the Usain Bolt of the sack race.*

WOULD YOU RATHER ?

only have a computer
or...
a tablet?

cry 7 times a week
or...
laugh for six hours
every day?

WOULD YOU RATHER ?

> get your favorite toy
> or...
> be your favorite
> superhero?

> be very good at math
> or...
> very good at sports?

WOULD YOU RATHER ?

be the actor of a
popular show
or...
a musician in a super
cool band?

live in the forest only
eating vegetables
or...
near the ocean only
eating fish?

WOULD YOU RATHER ?

have the ability to forge weapons out of thin air or...
the ability to change the color of any object you touch?

be a spy
or
be a ninja?

WOULD YOU RATHER ?

be able to control 6 random people
or...
only one specific person?

have feet for hands
or...
have hands for feet?

Did You Know...?

- *"Laughter is the best medicine", it can help you burn calories, relieve pain, boost your immune system and protect your heart.*

- *Fish contains multiple nutrients which are incredibly essential for your body, brain and vision, such as omega-3 fatty acids and vitamins such as D and B2. Fish is rich in phosphorus, calcium and is a great source of minerals, such as zinc, magnesium, potassium and iron.*

- *Eating fish at least two times per week as part of a healthy diet is recommended.*

WOULD YOU RATHER ?

be a main character in the Sims

or...

a professional basketball player?

meet your favorite actor

or...

be on your favorite TV show?

WOULD YOU RATHER ?

have two wings
or...
4 hands?

have belly button in
your forehead
or...
a belly button in
your chin?

WOULD YOU RATHER ?

sing in front of 100
people
or...
dance in front of 50
people

ride a T-Rex
or...
a unicorn?

WOULD YOU RATHER ?

be rich with no
friends
or...
be poor with a lot
of friends?

have the ability to see
from a very far distance
or...
be able to ride dolphins?

WOULD YOU RATHER ?

have the power to detect lies

or...

have the ability to make others believe whatever you say?

work on your homework during holidays

or...

do house chores?

Did You Know...?

- *The Quadrumana are certain type of monkeys and apes that have four hands, two attached to the arms and two attached to the legs*

- *Compared to other animals, dolphins are believed to be very intelligent. They have the longest memory in the animal kingdom.*
- *The average lifespan of a dolphin is 15 years. However, some of them have lived up to 50 years.*

- *According to mythology, if you touch a pure white unicorn, you will find happiness and joy throughout your entire life.*

WOULD YOU RATHER ?

have everyday be your birthday

or...

Christmas?

be a millionaire without fame

or...

popular with no money?

WOULD YOU RATHER ?

live a spaceship
or...
in a castle?

enter the cage of a
sleeping lion for 20
minutes
or...
swim across a river
infested with crocodiles?

WOULD YOU RATHER ?

eat only hot dogs for
the rest of your life
or...
only pizza?

spend 24 hours in
daylight
or...
night?

WOULD YOU RATHER ?

be able to read
people's mind
or...
move objects with
your mind?

be the world's
strongest person
or...
fastest person?

WOULD YOU RATHER ?

not cut your hair for
10 years
or...
not cut your fingernails
for 5 years?

take only cold
showers for a month
or...
sleep under the rain
for a week?

Did You Know...?

- In Svalbard, Norway, situated north of mainland Europe, the sun never sets every year from approximately the 19th of April to the 23rd of August.

- Usain Bolt is the fastest man in the world, his maximum speed has reached 27.44 miles/hour

- Nilanshi Patel, a 16-year-old girl from Gujarat, India, is the current record holder for the longest hair on a teenager. Nilanshi is also nicknamed Rapunzel. Her hair was measured at 170.5 cm (5 ft 7 in) in November 2018. She didn't have a haircut since she was 6 years old.

WOULD YOU RATHER ?

earn $100 after washing
the dishes for a week
or...
be given $50 after
changing 3 baby diapers?

always get up early
or...
always stay up late?

WOULD YOU RATHER ?

> *sleep with 100 mosquitos in your room or...*
> *50 tarantulas?*

> *never have to brush your teeth again or...*
> *never have to wash your face again?*

WOULD YOU RATHER ?

have an unlimited
supply of cheesecake
or...
ice cream?

have to wear your
pants backwards
or...
shoes on the wrong
feet?

WOULD YOU RATHER ?

live in a mountain cave with free *WIFI*
or...
a 5-stars hotel with no *WIFI*?

be the most powerful wizard
or...
the weakest superhero?

WOULD YOU RATHER ?

have to go to school
wearing a clown wig
or...
a clown nose?

have an giraffe-
sized rabbit
or...
a rabbit-sized bear?

Did You Know...?

- *Male mosquitoes never bite. It is the females that bites because it needs the proteins in blood to produce their eggs..*

- *82 days is the number of days a person spends brushing their teeth over a lifetime in the UK.*

- *Which Came First: Chocolate or Vanilla?*
- *The answer is chocolate, it was actually invented first. The creation of the first modern chocolate bar is credited to the Joseph Fry back in 1847.*

WOULD YOU RATHER ?

eat a spoonful of
mustard
or...
a raw egg?

eat a fried cricket
or...
a fried grasshopper
sandwich?

WOULD YOU RATHER ?

eat only popsicles
for a year
or...
cupcakes?

be able to talk to cats
or...
dogs?

WOULD YOU RATHER ?

give up cheese
or...
chocolate for the rest
of your life?

live on a sailboat
or...
in a wood cabin for
the rest of your life?

WOULD YOU RATHER ?

be Santa Clause
or...
the Tooth Fairy?

be able to roar like
a lion
or...
sing like a bird?

WOULD YOU RATHER ?

get tickled for 2 minutes
or...
take a shower with your clothes on?

be able to read lips
or...
learn sign language?

Did You Know...?

- *You Can't Tickle Yourself ! Why not?*
- *Essentially, we cannot surprise our own brain. Our brains are programmed to evade anticipated stimuli, including - perhaps most tellingly - tactile perceptions resulting from our own movements.*
- *Different Countries Have Different Sign Languages, there are over 130 sign languages.*
- *The Loudest Roar: A male lion has the loudest roar of any big cats species, it can be heard from up to five miles away.*
- *It takes 10L of milk to make just 1 pound (450g) of cheese*

WOULD YOU RATHER ?

tell all your secrets
or...
face all your fears?

have the ability to make
people dance every
time you sneeze
or...
rolling on the floor every
time you clap?

WOULD YOU RATHER ?

have everything you touch turn to gold

or...

to your favorite food?

own a talking gorilla

or...

have an alien be your best friend?

WOULD YOU RATHER ?

live in a place where
it always rains
or...
in the desert?

climb a mountain
wearing your slippers
or...
walk on ice barefoot?

WOULD YOU RATHER ?

have super strong legs
or...
super strong arms?

jump every time you
drink a glass of water
or...
spin in circles for 30
seconds ?

WOULD YOU RATHER ?

army crawl across
the room
or...
crab crawl across
the room?

live in a house built
from marshmallows
or...
a house built from
candy?

Did You Know...?

- *About a third of the Earth's surface is covered with deserts.*

- *Mount Everest is the world's highest mountain, Its peak reaches an incredible 8,848 metres (29,028 feet) above sea level*

- *When we stop spinning, the fluid inside our ears keeps spinning around. Your brain then receives the signal that your body continues to spin while your eyes send it the image of a stable environment. The result of this contradictory information confuse the brain into thinking we are still spinning. This is what causes us to feel dizzy!*

WOULD YOU RATHER ?

it was always winter
season
or...
summer season?

have bright green
hair
or...
a banana sized
earrings?

WOULD YOU RATHER ?

spend the night alone
in a haunted house
or...
be chased by a
zombie?

have the power to have
anything you order online
instantly delivered
or...
the ability to start a real life
Disney musical at any time?

WOULD YOU RATHER ?

always talk and act
like a robot

or...

have your finger always
stuck into your nose?

have the power to move
clouds and manipulate
their shape

or...

the ability to talk to
trees?

WOULD YOU RATHER ?

go fishing with your
fish-eating cat
or...
go camping with your
excessively barking dog?

be a cool villain
or...
a boring hero in a
movie?

WOULD YOU RATHER ?

have a unicorn horn
or...
have a horse's tail?

kiss a jellyfish
or...
hold a snake?

Did You Know...?

- *Jellyfish have no heart, brain, eyes or bones. Their smooth, bag-like body is mostly made up of water and tentacles armed with tiny, stinging cells.*

- *Darth Vader from Star Wars is considered one of the greatest villains of all time.*

- *Some scientists have claimed that a Zombie apocalypse could actually happen.*

- *Australia is considered the safest place if there was a Zombie apocalypse.*

- *Countries located within the equator will generally have "summer" all year round.*

WOULD YOU RATHER ?

be a famous singer
who can't dance
or...
a famous dancer who
can't sing?

eat a small can of
dog food
or...
eat three rotten
tomatoes?

WOULD YOU RATHER ?

have a monkey face
or...
a pig nose?

clean up after dinner
or...
set the table before
dinner?

WOULD YOU RATHER ?

jump into of a pool of mud
or...
a pool of chocolate pudding?

sneeze ice cream
or...
have your tears be cheese flavored?

WOULD YOU RATHER ?

eat two tablespoons
full of liquid soap
or...
drink a glass full of
salty water?

be an astronaut
or...
own a private plane?

WOULD YOU RATHER ?

have 500 grasshoppers in the rest of the house or...
100 spiders in your bedroom?

be good at every kind of sports or...
always get good grades?

Did You Know...?

- *Pigs have a keen sense of smell detecting food deep into ground roots with their very sensitive nose.*

- *Grasshoppers have six legs, a pair of antennas, four wings and small little pinchers to cut food which typically consists of grasses, leaves.*

- *If we drink salty water to quench our thirst, the kidneys have to use existing water from our body in order to dilute the extra salt, which in turn makes us feel even thirstier*

- *Our tears actually taste salty because they contain natural salts called electrolytes.*

WOULD YOU RATHER ?

have an unlimited amount of popcorn
or...
chips?

be able to play video games using only your mind
or...
be able to eat without using your hands?

WOULD YOU RATHER ?

get caught scratching
your privates
or...
get caught eating
a booger ?

have to use a public toilet
that has a snake in it
or...
one that it is dark and
extremely dirty?

WOULD YOU RATHER ?

*suffer from unpredictable
fainting spells
or...
from spontaneous loud
shouting?*

*start dancing every
time you sneeze
or...
rolling on the floor every
time you say "hi"?*

WOULD YOU RATHER ?

vacation somewhere
very cold
or...
very hot during the
holidays?

meet an alien
or...
meet a dinosaur?

WOULD YOU RATHER ?

*never have to
shower again
or...
never have to brush
your teeth again?*

*be able to stop time
or...
to go back to any
moment in your life?*

Did You Know...?

- *Boogers are a sign that your nose is functioning properly!*
- *Your nose produces about 1L of snot each day.*

- *A sneeze can travel up to 100 mph.*

- *Yes, it is possible to stop time. All you need to do is travel at light speed !*

- *It is believed that dinosaurs lived on Earth until around 65 million years ago when a mass extinction occurred.*

WOULD YOU RATHER ?

walk over a rainbow
or...
ride a shooting star?

raise lowing (mooing)
chickens
or...
raise clucking cows?

WOULD YOU RATHER ?

lose all your savings
or...
favorite toy?

fold all the clothes
or...
wash dirty clothes?

WOULD YOU RATHER ?

meet your future
grandchildren
or...
meet your ancestors?

be bitten by 30
mosquitoes
or...
be stung by a bee
7 times?

WOULD YOU RATHER ?

be stuck on a boat in the middle of the ocean
or...
a space rocket floating in space?

have a pet lion
or...
a pet bear?

WOULD YOU RATHER ?

swim in a pool of chocolate

or...

swim in a pool of ice cream?

be able to speak 7 different languages

or...

memorize the lyrics of every single song you hear?

Did You Know...?

- *Shooting stars are not actually stars! They are small rocks and dust penetrating the Earth's upper atmosphere at extremely high speeds.*

- *A "moonbow" is a lunar rainbow, an astonishing and rare phenomenon that can only occur at night under very specific conditions.*

- *Only female bees (queen and worker bees) can sting. A honey bee can only sting once, as barbs rip the stinger out of the bee and it will die. Bumblebee's and wasps stingers don't have barbs, so they can sting multiple times without injury.*

WOULD YOU RATHER ?

*throw confetti on everyone
you meet for a week
or ...
blow a horn every time
you meet someone?*

*not be able to talk
ever again
or...
only be able to yell
when you speak?*

WOULD YOU RATHER ?

be able to speak to animals

or...

speak every single human language?

be president of the United States

or...

be king or queen of another country?

WOULD YOU RATHER ?

travel through time
or...
travel around the
world?

eat three spiders
or...
eat a bowl full
of worms?

WOULD YOU RATHER ?

be able to breathe
underwater
or...
be able to fly?

become the size of
dinosaur
or...
be shrunk down to the
size of a bug?

WOULD YOU RATHER ?

see the future
or...
travel only back in
time?

become 10 years older
or...
5 years younger?

Did You Know...?

- *Humans lungs are not designed to be able to breathe underwater because there is not enough surface area inside the lungs to absorb enough oxygen from water.*

- *The sauropods were the largest and heaviest dinosaurs, reaching a length of 30 meters (98 ft.) and a weight of 88 tons.*

- *In certain cultures in Africa, Asia and Southern America, eating worms is considered a delicacy.*

- *Ferdinand Magellan, the portuguese explorer is often considered to be the first person to lead a crew to tour the world from 1519 to 1522.*

WOULD YOU RATHER ?

be the richest person
in the planet
or...
have three wishes
become true?

have a pet panda
or...
be a tiger tamer?

WOULD YOU RATHER ?

cough out a rat every
time you wheeze
or...
blow out 50 spider every
time you sneeze?

say out loud everything
that comes to your mind
or...
lose the ability to speak
unless someone spoke to
you?

WOULD YOU RATHER ?

live without air conditioning in the summer
or...
heating during winter?

sleep only two hours a day
or...
be awake only four hours a day for the rest of your life?

WOULD YOU RATHER ?

be able to talk without moving your lips
or...
see with your eyes closed?

get wrapped from head to toe in toilet paper
or...
put ice cubes down your shirt with your shirt tucked in?

WOULD YOU RATHER ?

*walk backwards
wherever you go
or...
walk on your hands?*

*hold an ice cube in your
hand until it melts
or...
sniff the pepper shaker?*

Did You Know...?

- *Jeff Bezos, the founder of Amazon is the richest man on the planet with an estimated net worth of 115 billion dollars.*

- *Kids aged between 6 to 12 years old are recommended to sleep from 9 to 12 hours a day.*

- *Pandas are an endangered species. Around 2000 pandas only are left living in the wild. Estimates may vary.*

- *The diet of a panda is made up almost entirely of bamboo.*

- *Pepper was so costly in earlier times that in ancient Rome and Greece, it was used as currency.*

Congratulations !

You succeeded at this ridiculous decision making challenge !

*I hope you had a fun time reading the book. If you enjoyed it, I would really appreciate if you leave us a review sharing your experience and stories. **It would mean a lot !!***

If you haven't done so already, make sure to check out my other books and follow my author's page on Amazon for future releases !

Till next time,
Witty Alfie

Witty Alfie
BONUS ACCESS

Join our fun club and get bonus monthly access to our giveaways & extras !

All you need to do is send us an email to WAPublishingGroup@gmail.com with the title "AMAZING ALFIE" – submit one ridiculous "Would You Rather..?" question and get :

- An entry to our monthly giveaway to win 50$ Amazon Gift Card !

- Access to our **free extras** !

A winner with the best submission will be picked each month and will be contacted via email.

Best of Luck !

Printed in Great Britain
by Amazon

59933236R00058